An Iskra Chapbook Series

LET US RISE
Trade Unionism in Ireland
Volume 2

Series Editor, **Róisín Dubh**

LET US RISE
Trade Unionism in Ireland
Volume 2

ORGANISING IN THE POST-PANDEMIC SPACE
Cristina Diamant

A ROUNDTABLE WITH WOMEN TRADE UNIONISTS
Róisín Dubh, Cristina Diamant, & Nora Labo

INTERVIEWS WITH ICELAND WORKERS
Róisín Dubh

WITH WRITINGS FROM
Mary Galway, Nora Connolly O'Brien, & Maud Eden

An Iskra Book

Published by Iskra Books 2024

All rights reserved.
The moral rights of the authors have been asserted.

Iskra Books
WWW.ISKRABOOKS.ORG
US | UK | Ireland

Iskra Books is an independent scholarly publisher—publishing original works of revolutionary theory, history, education, and art, as well as edited collections, new translations, and critical republications of older works.

ISBN-13: 979-8-8692-4836-7 (Chapbook)

British Library Cataloguing in Publication Data
A catalogue record for this book is available from the British Library

Library of Congress Cataloguing-in-Publication Data
A catalog record for this book is available from the Library of Congress

Cover Art and Design by Ben Stahnke
Typesetting by Róisín Dubh

Contents

Preface \ vi
Róisín Dubh

Organising in the Post-Pandemic Space \ 1
Cristina Diamant

Roundtable with Women Trade Unionists \ 25
Róisín Dubh, Cristina Diamant, and Nora Labo

Interviews with the Iceland Workers \ 49
Róisín Dubh

Trades Unions and Women's Employment \ 61
Mary Galway

"Woman's Place": Home or Factory? \ 73
Nora Connolly O'Brien

Two Roads for Irishwomen \ 81
Maud Eden

If it were possible for women to retire to their homes—BUT IT IS NOT!— civilisation as we know it, based on industrial development, would come crashing down, business would be in chaos [...]

—**Nora Connolly,** "Woman's Place": Home or Factory?

Preface

Róisín Dubh

In 2023, numerous labour uprisings occurred—and Ireland was not immune to this strike wave. Over the course of the months of September and October, 2023, a series of interviews were conducted with Independent Workers' Union (IWU) members involved in the high-profile Iceland Trade Dispute. In this volume, in addition to the workers' interviews, we include an essay from a member of the IWU, as well as three supporting, classic pieces written by Irishwomen Trade Unionists, including one from James Connolly's daughter, Nora, who proudly continued her father's work.

A recurring theme of the interviews present in this book is the presence of a large number of women, especially mothers, in the frontlines of Irish labor struggles. Taken together, classical writings from Irishwomen Trade Unionists and contemporary writings such as those from the Iceland workers, emphasize the ongoing, interconnected struggles of women who, across time, bear the brunt of exploitation. Women are providers for their families; they pay mortgages, and they have children to raise.

The present volume, the second in our *Let Us Rise: Trade Unionism in Ireland* series, reveals the voices of women in the Irish struggle; it also reveals the immense amount of union pride present among women workers. This volume works to demonstrate that, across time, there exists a deep solidarity among rank-and-file union members who know the power of the collective voice; who know that, as workers, we have, through struggle, nothing to lose but our chains.

Organising in the Post-Pandemic Space

Cristina Diamant

As president of the Independent Workers' Union (IWU), I am honoured to introduce the second volume of the *Let Us Rise* series of chapbooks on Irish Trade Unionism. The first volume in this series of Iskra chapbooks zeroed in on the particularities of the Irish working-class experience, particularly our analysis of the 2023 Iceland franchise industrial dispute alongside James Connolly's observations on capitalism in Ireland, which ring true louder than ever today. Our aim was to expose, through the Iceland struggle, the dehumanising conditions that are gradually being accepted as part and parcel of adult life—a nightmare divorced from fantasies of fairness fostered by the Irish government and its trade union partners.

The current volume insists on contradicting the assumption, parroted by politically compromised outlets, that workers have become complacent or that "nobody wants to work anymore." If there is anyone unwilling to face the facts, it is the members of the Irish Business and Employers Confederation (IBEC), deluding themselves into thinking that their backroom negotiations which keep workers' wages and benefits compressed will always be accepted unflinchingly and without building resentment. Effectively, what this series offers its readers is a mature perspective of-and-on working class life in Ireland; of workers who demand to have the value of their labour respected and treated with dignity. This is all the more important for women workers regularly subjected to baseless stereotypes of being temperamental, disproportionately concerned with supposedly frivolous issues, or distracted by the many challenges of domestic life and the caring duties expected of them.

More specifically, this volume is anchored in the experience of women working, writing, and organising in Ireland. In January 2024, a report by the Workplace Relations Commission (WRC) announced the recovery of approximately two million euro in unpaid or withheld wages in 2023, with almost 60% of these cases in the service and retail sector, disproportionately affecting women and immigrant workers.[1] In the IWU, we are sorely

---

[1] "Work Programme 2024," Workplace Relations Commission, accessed February 23, 2024, online at: https://www.work-

familiar with the limitations of the WRC, especially how often these very same wronged workers are verbally intimidated in the workplace and reminded to count their blessings—left without a consistent paper trail of the many injustices against them. Often, this uphill battle may feel like a time sink and a burden too heavy to carry over months on the waitlist until adjudication, a time of intense stress and often attempts at coercion, if not outright retaliation or victimisation. When these very same workers have loved ones depending on their time, attention, and energy, it is no wonder that even the dire image presented by the WRC report can only be an incomplete picture of the true scale of injustice in the workplace.

Indeed, when labour inspectors are rarer than quality inspectors as the integrity of the product is valued over the dignity of the worker in capitalism, it should be no wonder that WRC figures only show the tip of the iceberg. Even self-assessed figures such as those of the 2020 *Working to the Bone* report published by the Migrant Workers Rights Centre suffer from the same issue: for exhausted and underappreciated workers, time is a valuable resource, making it difficult to see the value of embarking on the long and arduous task of fighting

---

placerelations.ie/en/publications_forms/corporate_matters/wrc-work-programme-2024.pdf.

back.[2] Workers are vastly undervalued in the gig economy, as we have seen with the 2024 Valentine's Day strike initiated by Deliveroo migrant workers, who are even further divided both geographically and by the very nature of contract work, where they are set against each other for the same dwindling pool of customers in a cost of living crisis.

A timely reminder of how to effectively counter the steady degradation of working conditions comes from Jane F. McAlevey's 2016 *No Shortcuts: Organizing for Power in the New Gilded Age*, where she points out that "the unions that still use the strike weapon [...] are also the unions whose members are negotiating—and gaining—contracts with life-altering improvements. Many of them are situated in the new service economy, which is dominated by women, often women of color. Those workers understand that their jobs cannot easily be shipped abroad or automated—yet."[3] Even when a supermarket installs self-service tills, the workers are not replaced so much as displaced. They now have to supervise the customers using

---

[2] "Working to the Bone: The Experiences of Migrant Workers in the Meat Sector in Ireland," Migrant Rights Centre Ireland, published November 30, 2020, online at: https://www.mrci.ie/2020/11/30/working-to-the-bone.

[3] Jane F. McAlevey, *No Shortcuts: Organizing for Power in the New Gilded Age* (New York: Oxford University Press, 2016), 27.

the tills, intervene swiftly, then step back again and restock merchandise. While the Iceland franchise had never implemented this system, avoiding the initial cost of introducing new technology, it was at the expense of unknowingly allowing workers and customers to continue to have a very direct, a very human interaction.

The above observation also ties in with McAlevey's point on the necessity of having trade unions' "organizing methods [...] deeply embedded in, and reliant on, an understanding of workers in relationship to the communities in which they lived."[4] Truly, it is this principle that we credit for the stalwart determination and support for the Talbot Street Iceland staff when the IWU organised rallies and sit-ins, alternating shifts to temporarily relieve the workers occupying the store themselves. What is more, this principle is alien to the neoliberal establishment, which prefers to pretend that issues affecting workers in the workplace are atomised and individual, even isolated from the fabric of public life.

Naturally, we contest such a view. Deteriorating working conditions in one sector of the industry concern us all, both as workers and as members of the community. We saw this not too long ago in our organising work in county Cork as well. Here,

---

4 Ibid. 27.

we recall Jack Horgan-Jones and Hugh O'Connell's 2022 *Pandemonium: Power, Politics and Ireland's Pandemic* pointing out how "[m]eat plants were the perfect breeding ground for COVID. As with nursing homes, the virus found a weak point, and ruthlessly took advantage."[5] Unsurprisingly, just as the two aforementioned reports had also indicated, "[m]any of the workers were non-Irish nationals, sharing accommodation and transport, insulated by language and cultural barriers from wider public health messaging"[6] and, just as we had seen in our work through the Cork Operative Butchers' Branch of the IWU, "[t]hey were poorly paid, with bad terms and conditions, and in the absence of sick pay arrangements, they were often forced to work when they were sick in order to send money home or support themselves,"[7] all while the official message was that "the measure was to stop the virus 'getting into the community.'"[8] The classic neoliberal advice, calling dissatisfied workers to simply find another job falls flat here: where else do you go when so many employers, all members of IBEC, start lowering wages and benefits at the same time?

---

5 Jack Horgan-Jones and Hugh O'Connell, *Pandemonium: Power Politics and Ireland's Pandemic* (Dublin: Gill Books, 2022), 167.

6 Ibid. 165.

7 Ibid. 165.

8 Ibid. 167.

We are often told that workers must demonstrate a genuine enthusiasm for their work, looking beyond compensation. Here in Ireland, just as in the United States or elsewhere, they already do, as McAlevey observes that "bribes didn't work: money wasn't what the workers were looking for,"[9] but dignified treatment and "the right to negotiate rules governing safety, hours, and similar issues."[10] Unorganised workers are not simply vulnerable to hazards, but often penalised by suffering the ill effects of their experience with said hazard. Even after a pandemic, too many employers are in no rush to invest in their workers' safety. In our experience, it is a struggle to reach even the first two levels in the hierarchy of controls for safety in the workplace, namely obtaining PPE (Personal Protective Equipment) fit for purpose and implementing administrative controls that change the way people work. We have much left to do, from making sure that each workplace has a Health and Safety Committee which includes workers to going up the hierarchy of controls for safety, exploring options such as engineering controls (which remove people from the hazard), substitution (which replaces the hazard identified), and finally to elimination (where hazards are removed entirely).

---

9   McAlevey, 33.

10   McAlevey, 32.

Re-defining the Narrative

We have continually found that we cannot rely on the media to engage with workers fairly and without bias towards "well-behaved" unions involved in social partnership power brokering and employers. The 2021 article published by *The Guardian* covering the IWU industrial dispute with AA Euro, a recruitment agency which registered its workers in Poland despite working in Ireland, failed to present the workers' grievances in a dignified manner while framing the IWU organiser's comments in clipped quotes that removed valuable context for their struggle and its relevance for all workers in Ireland.[11] Unsurprisingly, the establishment has a stake in presenting such issues, no matter how widespread, as a simple and temporary malfunctioning of capitalism. However, when the employers organise to lobby for the same policies, it must be exposed as a bug rather than a feature.

As a trade union, we are tasked with dispelling many of the illusions workers are asked to entertain about the role of capitalism despite ample, everyday evidence to the contrary. Here, I would like to introduce a key concept coined by Stafford Beer,

---

[11] Ella McSweeney and Holly Young, "The invisible migrant workers propping up Ireland's €4bn meat industry," *The Guardian*, published September 28, 2021, online at: https://www.theguardian.com/environment/2021/sep/28/the-invisible-migrant-workers-propping-up-irelands-4bn-meat-industry.

a professor at the Manchester Business School active on issues such as management cybernetics and operational research. It is a remarkably simple principle that cuts across through all the contradictions outlined above. Professor Beer indicates that the purpose of a system is what it does, not what it declares as its purpose yet consistently fails to achieve in practice.[12] This is why this volume offers no rose-tinted view: we are looking plainly at the facts and at what the establishment continues to do, whether it wants to admit it or not. In practice, it silences workers so that it can continue to treat them as disposable "human resources," no different than any other piece of equipment necessary to keep operations running.

Precisely because we have set out to speak plainly about the facts of the matter, I have invited my former colleague, Nora Labo, who represented IWU members in front of the special Oireachtas committee of safety in the workplace in the summer of 2020 to speak in her own words about her experience as a woman in the trade union movement; similarly, in 2021, I invited the leader of the AA Euro workers in Shannon Vale, Daniela Mitran, to speak on her experience as a woman working in Ireland and active in the trade union movement alongside a Romanian labour lawyer representing

---

12   Stafford Beer, "What is cybernetics?" *Kybernetes*, Vol. 31 No. 2, pp. 209-219.

immigrants in the service sector in South Italy for the Contracurent channel—recognising that exploitative and extractive labour practices are not confined to a single country or industry sector.

Continuing A Tradition of Women Leading Labour

With this occasion, I want to thank many of the inspiring and fearless women I have met in the all-island (Ireland) trade union movement, especially Lynda Walker from Belfast and Margaret Healy from the Home Helps branch of the IWU, demonstrating over years that no matter how much the rich and powerful can try to intimidate us, women can be a force to be reckoned with.

My introduction is also a nod to *Phenomenal Women: A Decade of Action* (2021), edited by Lynda Walker with Helen Crickard, Anne McVicker, and Danielle Roberts—a remarkable volume addressing disappointing and insufficient policies across the border—documenting the struggle of women from all backgrounds for better conditions, from the first reported events organised on this island for International Working Women's Day to Reclaim the Night and, more recently, to Reclaim the Agenda—showing that feminism is not a mere theoretical framework relegated to the 60s and the 70s or even to a single location—it is a living practice of community-building with others. Notable here is the decades-long collaboration between Lynda Walker and Angela Davis.

Prison labour is yet another form of labour exploitation and political disenfranchisement that is becoming worryingly common, especially as more American states criminalise being homeless or as the UK ramps up its monitoring of activists. Far-right violence is on the rise, and the IWU recently pledged to endorse the ten foundational principles of Le Cheile DND (Diversity Not Division) showing unwavering support for migrant workers. Amidst this tense political climate, Ireland is holding a polarising referendum on International Women's Day that is worrying many workers in the Home Help sector as it coincides with the staggered closure of a significant number of nursing homes, making them fear that caring duties will slowly not only be privatised, but also offloaded onto the family instead of being kept as a public service. As IWU stressed in our 2023 International Women's Day statement, regardless of age, ability or background, we all deserve to be safe at work, in the streets, and at home.

Our work is unavoidably tied to reclaiming the working class origins of International Working Women's Day as an opportunity to celebrate and continue our fight rather than rest on symbolic laurels. Clara Zetkin, who proposed celebrating working women at the 1910 Second International Conference of Working Women, stressed two key principles: only with women will all workers win, and only with all workers will women win; economic, social, and political rights go hand in hand—losing one makes the entire edifice collapse like a house of cards even as marketers today attempt to shrewdly exploit the day for profit. Workers do not simply want bread and women do not simply want the occasional International Women's Day roses. We want more than a life crushed between expanding caring needs as our social support is weakened and our services are sold out piecemeal to the private sector. As our Home Help branch members have noted over the years, we are now facing a working life with both longer and longer hours and a rising age of retirement.

However, we cannot afford to wallow in despair or be paralysed into inaction. Instead, what we need is revolutionary hope. We recall the famous 1911 poem that inspired the song often heard on International Working Women's Day:

> As we go marching, marching, unnumbered women dead
> Go crying through our singing their ancient call for bread.
> Small art and love and beauty their drudging spirits knew.
> Yes, it is bread we fight for, but we fight for roses, too.
> [...]
> No more the drudge and idler, ten that toil where one reposes,

But a sharing of one's glories.
Bread and roses, bread and roses.
Our lives shall not be sweated from birth until life closes;
Hearts starve as well as bodies; bread and roses, bread and roses.[13]

We must stress that Clara Zetkin, imprisoned in Germany for her anti-war activities just like her friend and comrade Rosa Luxemburg, recognised how intimately connected capitalism and imperialist violence are, a truth we are aware of as keenly today. In a time when the right wing tries to distract and divide across lines of ethnicity or belief, we are proud to stand firm with a tradition of international class solidarity.

A Woman's Place is in a Union

Our work as women within the union movement is not reduced t.o that of personal assistants or secretaries; rather, we take initiative as educators, agitators, organisers. We do not act in place of the workers, but empower them to make a positive change themselves as they are the experts on their own working conditions. As anyone who has worked for the Iceland franchise or has attended

---

13   James Oppenheim, "Bread and Roses," in *The Cry For Justice: An Anthology of the Literature of Social Protest*, Upton Sinclair, ed., John C. Winston Co., 1915, accessed March 12, 2024, online at: https://www.marxists.org/subject/women/poetry/bread.html

our rallies in support of the Iceland campaign already knows, one worker in particular was taking charge, having earned the trust of her coworkers. With this occasion, we would like to thank Donna Grimes for speaking out for her fellow workers on countless occasions, including at our 2023 Annual Delegate Congress and with Mebh McDaid from Trademark Belfast for *This Week at Work* podcast.[14]

The bubbling force of the trade union movement seeks to reach the surface, where it erupts as a sudden disruption for employers, but a welcome release for workers, who are now able to speak in one voice—demanding an improvement in working conditions, thus leading to an increased quality of work, which could no longer be as easily dismissed as substandard. This issue is especially widespread in light industry, such as the garment sector, which has been historically dominated by women workers. Wage deductions become less frequent once proper instruction and equipment is guaranteed. If it seems impractical to maintain a system where workers are essentially set up to fail, leading to both customer and worker dissatisfaction for the sake of short-term savings, it is because this is simply one of the many contradictions of capitalism. Here, we

---

14 Mebh McDaid, "141. Climate Change, Iceland Strike and Cluster Bombs," July 19, 2023, in *This Week at Work*, podcast, https://irepod.com/podcast/the-week-at-work/141-climate-change-iceland-strike-and-cluster-bomb.

are returning to one of the issues identified in the foreword of the first volume: just as quality inspectors are necessary to ensure the quality of a product or service, labour inspectors are sorely needed on a regular basis to diagnose the root cause instead of simply allowing workers to be blamed for being the face of its symptoms.

However, real change does not come from the sporadic intervention of inspectors. Once, when I was called on to act as a Romanian interpreter during an inspection in a factory in county Cork, a worker told me as an aside that they all wish for more frequent inspections, clarifying that work was always more manageable with inspectors around. Staffing numbers during an inspection eased the usual pressure, while each worker was also ordered to process fewer units per minute than usual. Indeed, even the conveyor belt was set to a speed that decreased user error and physical strain, making it less likely for workers to have their pay docked in case a product fell off the alarmingly fast conveyor belt. The day-to-day reality on the ground was very different, with repetitive strain injury being one of the chief causes of missed work or missed KPIs (key performance indicators). All of this made for a very strange image: managers seemed to be the only ones anxious about the inspection, while the workers saw it as a brief respite from unrealistic standards of productivity they had complained about repeatedly only to feel inadequate.[15] The keyword here is *pressure*: for change to take root in the workplace, what is needed is constant pressure exercised on the shopfloor by workers adamant that this cannot go on.

Turning now to the writings of Irish trade union women featured in this volume, Mary Galway gave evidence in 1908 before a House of Commons-appointed committee and in 1911 on the spread of disease. Galway's voice belongs to a lineage of women in the trade union movement taking policymakers to task, much like our own Nora Labo did in 2020 on behalf of IWU members.[16] War, much like epidemics, reliably proves how essential workers are in keeping the world running as usual, while in times of peace and relative prosperity, they are presumed to be easily replaceable once worn down and worn out.

Having established the keen perspective of

---

15 Nora Labo, "Killing twelve chickens a minute—Some thoughts on organising in Irish meat plants," *Left East*, published May 29, 2020, online at: https://lefteast.org/killing-twelve-chickens-a-minute-some-thoughts-on-organising-in-irish-meat-plants/

16 Nora Labo, Letter to Aileen Fallon- Clerk to the "Special Committee on Covid-19 Response," sent June 16, 2020, online at: https://data.oireachtas.ie/ie/oireachtas/committee/dail/33/special_committee_on_covid_19_response/submissions/2020/2020-09-30_submission-daniel-snihur-independent-workers-union-scc19r-r-0246_en.pdf

women workers in industries men are less present and thus often less aware of, let us now address the supposed conflict between men workers and women workers. Rather counterintuitively, the common argument goes that the element of danger is not the risk of harassment or bullying too many women are still confronted with on a daily basis, but that women are undermining the men by charging less for their labour. In effect, this is an inversion of the real power relation: it is the employer who underpays the worker, much the same way that it is not the immigrant who drives wages down. Instead, it is a case of employers noticing and exploiting workers' limited options and their urgent need for stability; and this is important to keep in mind in times when people are displaced by conflict, disease, and climate change alike.

There is also the hidden phenomenon of underemployment that runs secondary to brain drain. Sometimes, resentment between workers builds up from the perception that experienced male workers are not rewarded for their loyalty, while the newcomers in the industry (not uncommonly women admitted in the sector for the first time) have to be incentivised with a higher wage to join the workplace. However, this is not a sign of incoming women workers supposedly having more economic power than the older workers. Once again, let us accurately name this: this is wage compression.

Employers are aware how costly the process of applying for a new role is for workers, and they do not need to incentivise older workers to stay. At the same time, older workers are often unaware how expensive the recruitment process is and how powerful they would be if they all demanded their length of service to be rewarded accordingly.

This is exactly what Nora Connolly O'Brien tackles head on in "Woman's Place: Home or Factory? The Limits of Change," where she points out the double standard of claiming in one breath that a woman's place is in the home, while also paying her a different rate, usually a lower one out of the assumption that caring duties will make her an unreliable worker. This is a surprisingly topical point, especially as this volume is released the year of a rather unusual referendum accused of confused messaging about its stakes. The timing of the current constitutional debate about "a woman's place" is also mired in controversy during a housing crisis when many workers are at risk of losing their homes despite there being more vacant buildings than people supported by temporary accommodation and homeless shelters.[17] Still reeling after a pandemic where too many women were caught

---

17 Housing Ireland, "Repurposing vacant homes can reduce homelessness," published July 18, 2023, online at: https://housingireland.ie/repurposing-vacant-homes-can-reduce-homelessness/

between a rock and a hard place, unable to leave an abusive home for fear of homelessness, but also stuck with their aggressors in a confined place, we are left to question the very term "shelter in place."

Indeed, Nora Connolly O'Brien illustrates the true cost of these caring duties, from housework to medical assistance. There is an infrastructure that benefits society as a whole. It is much too easy to call it priceless labour and perhaps equally dangerous to try to price it, as Silvia Federici's "Wages for Housework Campaign" showed how quickly this would price most people out of these taken for granted services. Nora Connolly O'Brien lamenting how those "who desire to marry have no prospect of a home save a room in a slum" rings uncomfortably familiar, especially as she identifies it not as an isolated, personal failing but lays the blame squarely at the feet of policymakers hypocritically prioritising their own pockets as "[o]ur Christian municipalities having decreed that slum clearance shall be a staple Irish industry." Decreasing living standards are connected to an increasingly limited access to healthcare, all but officially paywalled in Ireland, as shown in Sara Burke's 2009 *Irish Apartheid: Healthcare Inequality in Ireland*. There should be no surprise that this is yet another issue that goes hand in hand with a marked preference for empty gestures for essential workers during a crisis instead of a living wage that can afford them the stability and dignity they deserve. Moreover, Nora Connolly O'Brien also takes issue with the false promise of so-called "feminine" jobs in education and care, calling them "a red herring to draw men off the scent" so that they may not notice that they are exploited not because of female workers but right alongside them. I would like to add here that the process of gendering occupations[18] is a highly-charged ideological one constantly updated throughout history and that wages tend to fall in the sectors men flee while the jobs now represented by a majority of female workers also lose status as this happens. This is precisely why we insist on speaking of better working conditions for all.

Last but certainly not least, Maud Eden speaks of trade unions in conjunction with republicanism, asking the crucial question: "If we dislike domination in politics, why accept it in Labour affairs?" We cannot allow our hopes for the future to be limited by the constraints of the present, no matter how used to them we have become. They are neither natural nor inevitable, as the science fiction writer Ursula le Guin also pointed out:

> We live in capitalism. Its power seems inescapable. So did the divine right of kings. Any human power can be resisted and changed by human beings. Resistance and change often begin in art, and very often in our art, the

---

18 Amanda Wilkerson, "So wives didn't work in the 'good old days'? Wrong," *The Guardian*, published April 13, 2014.

art of words.[19]

In truth, the purpose of the present volume is to remind us that these are not impossible or absurd demands. We have worked towards them before and they can be achieved anew, both on this island and abroad. However, to do so we must stay resolute in our fight for a better tomorrow and not accept empty symbolism as a half-measure. I want us to recall here James Connolly pointing out the hypocrisy of hoisting up the green flag while allowing imperialist economic exploitation to continue, effectively meaning that:

> England will still rule you. She would rule you through her capitalists, through her landlords, through her financiers, through the whole array of commercial and individualist institutions she has planted in this country and watered with the tears of our mothers and the blood of our martyrs.[20]

This point brings us back full circle to the post-Brexit political and economic landscape, as we have seen exactly what this means when British retailers have started to leave the Irish market:

---

19 Ursula K. Le Guin, qtd. in "Ursula K. Le Guin burns down the National Book Awards," *Portland Monthly*, published November 20, 2014, online at: https://www.pdxmonthly.com/arts-and-culture/2014/11/ursula-k-le-guin-rocks-the-national-book-awards-november-2014

20 James Connolly, "Socialism and Nationalism," published January 1897, online at: https://www.marxists.org/archive/connolly/1897/01/socnat.htm

first Debenhams,[21] then Argos and Iceland. As I draw nearer to my conclusion, I also want to thank Debenhams workers for their relentless support during the Iceland industrial dispute, especially as they were undoubtedly the canaries in the coal mine. They quickly realised that Iceland workers were next on the chopping block, first fed reassuring platitudes while cold calculations were made behind their backs. Unionising is also a matter of fostering lasting ties with fellow workers, even as one may change jobs or relocate. What makes the difference between hopelessness and daring to hope for justice is a durable network of people who share the courage to dream fearlessly together and act towards making those dreams the new reality. To do so, one also needs the courage to name the issues in your workplace. The problems that are both widely felt and deeply felt are the first few visible wins necessary to build momentum towards creating a movement. This is a marathon, not a sprint, and we stress in our roundtable how crucial it is to create a network so as to avoid burnout and despair.

We sincerely hope that this volume will be a valuable tool for yourself, your colleagues, and your loved ones. Seek other women in the workplace and bring them into the trade union movement.

---

21 Sue O'Connell and Fergus Dowd, "Tales from the Debenhams Picket Line," accessed March 4, 2024, online at: https://www.debspickettales.ie.

Never allow yourselves or your employers to underestimate your power when united. May this volume equip you with the knowledge and confidence that with enough energy and a sense of the urgency of our struggle, we have a world to win. After all, a better world is not only possible, but urgently necessary for us all.

Roundtable Discussion with Women Trade Unionists
Conducted December 2023

Róisín Dubh, Cristina Diamant, & Nora Labo

W*hat was your impression of community organising and trade unions before getting involved? What values did you associate with them and what kind of demographic?*

RÓISÍN: I was raised in a union household. I grew up with my grandfather and father both being in the union. From birth, my father stressed I should have a union job. Also, from a young age, I have been involved with community organising. I have had nothing but positive impressions, because I knew both helped the working class, my people.

CRISTINA: For my family, a union job meant stability and some level of protection from lay-offs, especially in the context of deindustrialisation in the 1990s in Eastern Europe. I'd say the teachers' union is the main union that hasn't been successfully fully demonised quite yet because education is seen as a public good. It helped that I knew early on that I wanted to be involved in education and that I first got a taste of this kind of work when I became a student representative, then a Student Union President. However, I was very disappointed to see a lot of my fellow representatives act as if we were in a sort of bubble and that, once we graduated, we were expected to each fend for ourselves without any awareness of how we are all impacted by the same conditions.

NORA: I actually started getting involved with organising work in France rather than in my home country, Romania, because I arrived in France when I started college. I have lived in working class migrant neighbourhoods in the Paris *banlieue* (suburb), close to shanty towns, and I gradually understood first hand, by talking and becoming friends with some of the people, mostly Romanian Roma migrants, who were living there, the true breadth of housing, education and health inequalities in one of the world's wealthiest cities. I found it really important to stand together with them and support their voice in the long-term, beyond just the occasional individual cases, for example, when their children were excluded from schools. In organising with these communities, I saw the centrality of housing justice to ensuring access to other rights as well. When you live in precarious accommodation, or are subject to repeated evictions, it is difficult to access social security supports, keep children in school, attend regular medical treatments etc. This later also came up when we were organising meat plant workers with the Independent Workers' Union (IWU) first, as their accommodation was conditional on their job, with their employer being also their de facto landlord, which created a threat for workers' housing security when they spoke up at their jobs, and vice versa. This was a very salient case where made labour and housing struggles were entwined and emphasised the need for trade unions and housing organising to work hand in hand, something we also worked on developing within the Community Action Tenants' Union (CATU) during my time as a CATU regional organiser.

CRISTINA: I've noticed that a lot of workers who came here, often through an agency, assumed that everything that was different in Ireland compared to the other countries they'd worked in was a whole package, essentially, and that you had to either accept it or leave. A lot of times I've had to explain that no, what you are complaining about isn't even compliant with Irish employment law and yes, you are allowed to point it out. All workers benefit if you do! Irish trade unions aren't only for Irish citizens, and they're not even restricted to EU citizens only. If you're a resident here and you work here, you are part of the demographic for an Irish trade union. It's sometimes difficult to get that across when trade unions aren't really featured in the Irish press as much as elsewhere, like in the United Kingdom, where they are seen as disruptive rather than in partnership with employers.

NORA: Exactly. I had naively expected conditions to be less brutal for migrant workers in Ireland compared to, say, France, where there was quite openly violent state repression against migrants especially in terms of detention and deportations. However, in Ireland I feel the economic and social violence, while different, is shocking in its breadth, and trade unions have more limited means than elsewhere (no solidarity strikes allowed, for instance). Before getting involved in the IWU, I'd never really been active in a trade union, simply because I'd only had very precarious short-term jobs in small workplaces (like market stalls for instance). Generally, I'd say my perception was that trade unions were mostly made of older people in more stable jobs, really, the kind of industrial or public sector jobs where you tend to see your coworkers every day. But yes, I always believed that collective organising is the way to go, and anecdotally I was once involved in a wild cat strike where we shut down the entire shop I worked in. We were only five people, and it felt like a revelation that we could do it and get what we wanted within two hours. I think in general when I arrived in Ireland, I had already seen the huge capacity to collectively mobilise in French trade unions, and many examples of collective action getting the goods. In France, I had also been involved in solidarity with migrant prisoner struggles, an experience which taught me how visas and work permits, or the lack thereof, are used to blackmail workers into putting up with unbearable exploitation. We also saw this with our meat plant workers in the IWU, who had been de facto made into undocumented persons through sham contracts and were thus at the mercy of their employers for even the smallest administrative needs, like getting proof of address to open a bank account.

What made you want to get involved with community organising and/or trade unions? What do you think about your experience?

RÓISÍN: I have always felt like it was a duty to help the working class, and to be involved with union work. My experiences have lived up to my expectations, while the work is difficult, when you can help even one person, it means the world. Obviously, I would change it so everyone is in a union with strong protections from the ruling class.

CRISTINA: To be honest, I got into organising somewhat reluctantly. I already had a lot of respect for trade union representatives, but I assumed you had to already be in a pretty stable professional position yourself first and I wasn't. I was teaching in short-term and isolated contexts, such as for a summer school or 1-on-1 tuition through a remote agency. The English as a Foreign Language (EFL) sector is a bit of a blind spot for trade unions, as many qualified people drift in and out of different schools, all privately owned and in competition with one another for the same pool of international students. It's very difficult, then, to form bonds of trust. I was first brought into the IWU in 2017 by my best friend as a Romanian translator and interpreter. I didn't think I could help myself, but I knew I wanted to help migrant workers.

NORA: As I was saying earlier, I got involved with organising because I feel no positive social change can be enacted without putting the voices and agency of those who are most oppressed at the core of our struggles. To me, real solidarity can only exist when we all work together on an equal footing, building collective movements, not in the unequal dynamics of charity and advocacy, in which hierarchies of class and class-dependent expertise are reinforced, and which end up being disempowering for those they supposedly "help."

When I first came to Ireland in 2019, what I noticed was a widespread resignation that people had in relation to their work conditions, a kind of disbelief with the idea that workers might actually have agency and collective power. And also, a notion among regular Irish people (and not only) that Ireland is a place with decent wages, relatively acceptable work conditions, overall ok. At the same time, I soon discovered there were thousands of migrant workers who lived like ghosts, they were completely invisible in the country, cheated out of social security, benefits, pensions, working illegally long hours in physically dangerous conditions. This was compounded by the severe legal restrictions on trade union action, as compared to most other EU countries.

CRISTINA: I think that's a great way to phrase it: it's not just that they were not being heard or that they were isolated, but a lot of times they weren't really seen by the system, either. We've had a case, for example, where the agency was not declaring their income to Revenue, but it was paying tax for them in the country the agency was active. The workers didn't even find out that they were invisible to the Irish state until they developed health issues on the job and found out that they weren't entitled to sick pay despite working for years, often without even taking annual leave. The IWU was able to inform them about their rights so that they could issue their demands themselves.

NORA: What I noticed was that the most active and valuable organising work was often done by very determined women workers, even though they made up only a small percentage of the workers in a meat plant, a traditionally male environment. What I found interesting is that even the process of recruiting them was very gendered from the beginning.

CRISTINA: Even retention was often gendered, too, often combined with work that was not on the same level as their own qualifications or experience. There was a case where a Romanian woman was offered a better job elsewhere as an interpreter, but she had to stay on in the factory to support her husband and her son because she was effectively acting as their translator and interpreter. It only made sense then for her to become the shop steward, as she was already very ambitious and knowledgeable. Going back to your point on recruitment, though, you went in person to the agency yourself, didn't you?

NORA: Yes, I wanted to see for myself what these workers were promised, so I flew back to my hometown where the agency had an office. From the very beginning, the agency insisted that I couldn't sign a contract as a single woman because they only signed up women who were ready to leave with their partner or their husband. They would simply never allow a woman to work alone. Beyond exposing the agency's shocking view of women as individuals lacking autonomy, only to be employed if accompanying a man, what that also told me was that, even though they'd never admit it openly, they couldn't vouch for your safety, especially in the accommodation they provided.

CRISTINA: While we're all aware on some level that companies over promise during the interview stage, it was quite shocking how badly they could underdeliver on said promises.

NORA: It also suited the agency to sign up couples even over single men. They could then book one room for a couple in a shared house, but charge each of them as much as they would normally charge a single man with his own room. To go back to the point you made about underemployment, I noticed it was a widespread issue among the women workers we organised. Even though many women were qualified butchers in Romania and had official qualifications, they were still only signed up on the General Operative rate, which is lower. It's no surprise then that these women were very vocal, oftentimes more so than the men that came with them. I think it's also an effect of gendered socialising. If you were brought up in a patriarchal context, you could see a lot of men have too much pride and fear of ridicule from their male colleagues to ever complain about their working conditions or be the first to suggest the idea of unionising before it becomes popular. On the other hand, women are socialised to mediate conflicts, and nurture informal networks of sociability and solidarity, which is hard work that often goes undervalued.

CRISTINA: I think we both have in mind the way in which wage theft comes with its own level of humiliation and fear of retaliation if you speak up. There was even a recent report showing that the Workplace Relations Commission (WRC) had to recover almost 2 million euro from employers in 2023, a good percentage of these cases coming from the food sector and the service sector. Who knows how many more cases have gone unreported so far? You could never claim to "forget" to pay a supplier properly, but that happens all the time to workers. The ones most affected were precisely women, younger people, and migrant workers, so everyone who is expected not to complain and simply go on with business as usual.

NORA: This is exactly what I'd like to see change. Too many of these very strong-willed women were also on the receiving end of a lot of sexism in the workplace, even from some of their own fellow workers. This happened especially when negotiations for pay rises went wrong and the men would blame them as if they had voluntarily given in. What is more, men sometimes dismissed their concerns as not essential to the struggle, especially if it was a gendered concern raised as a demand, where the women hoped they could count on support from fellow workers of any gender (for instance lack of privacy in locker rooms). We are always more successful when we stand together.

Once you became active in community organising and/or a trade union, how did your impression change? What assumption(s) would you like to challenge?

RÓISÍN: It is definitely time-consuming work which I had not realised, and some people, no matter how much you educate, will be resistant. I do want those who think the working class are inherently right wing to know how completely wrong they are.

NORA: To be honest, when a friend recommended I help migrant workers through the Independent Workers' Union in Cork, I was a bit apprehensive because I had this perception of Irish trade unions being too much of an old boys' club, so to say, yet at the same time much milder in their demands than continental trade unions.

CRISTINA: I think it's important to keep in mind the distinction between service unions and fighting unions. Otherwise, it can easily feel like you can only find militant unions in France and that all Irish unions are establishment unions that only sign people on, take on a case with the WRC and don't pose a challenge to any employer no matter how much they mistreat their employees. This brings me back to your previous point, on how establishment unions negotiate with the government and the employers because they want to be seen as part of the system. This means that they will not want to remove themselves from these structures of power by bringing up anything uncomfortable, but this only further alienates the workers, who do not feel represented. Of course, not talking about this distinction only benefits service unions as they like to pretend that this is the only way Irish trade unions can act, which is so far from the truth.

NORA: My criticism at the time was also that the trade union movement seemed to be lagging behind on a number of social issues, such as gendered discrimination in the workplace or LGBT+ issues. I also felt that, compared to the context I'd seen in France for instance, in Ireland there was minimal organising on newer contexts of labour exploitation, such as gig economy workers or jobseekers who are on Community Employment. It's such a well-developed sector but there's not much autonomy one can have on such a scheme where they're paid pitiful wages for their work.

CRISTINA: I see what you mean. I'm afraid it's a double whammy of both Thatcherite and Reaganite influences, which is a pity given the hopes James Connolly or Mother Jones had both for the Irish trade union movement and for the international trade union movement.

NORA: This is why it was a bit of a shock in the beginning to see so much of the Irish trade union movement start again with the ABCs, having to go over why unionising is important. Even if you were to look elsewhere, like at social movements, you would still come up against the same issue where those most exploited were denied expertise in their own lives and other people wanted to speak for, or rather, over them. While I'd like to see sexism called out in a more targeted way everywhere, the IWU was the most radical option, so I'd like to challenge the idea that trade unions can only be mild and non-confrontational.

How has the trade union movement changed during the time you were active?

RÓISÍN: It has exploded! I got my start 20 or so years ago, and it has done nothing but grown! I would stress on younger people if they are getting discouraged that we are in a much better position than we were decades ago. The working class is hungry for change, and we need to be there with them.

NORA: At first, I have to admit I wasn't too hopeful about the success we'd have organising Romanian and Moldovan workers because of how strong anti-left broadly and, by extension, anti-trade union propaganda has been in Eastern Europe since the 1990s. Thus, it would have probably been difficult to motivate them had we chosen an abstract political or ideological stance as an entry point, but instead it worked really well to organise around the material issues of their daily lives, and thus illustrate the value of collective organising through the very process of the struggle, rather than theoretical arguments. I am more hopeful now both for the Irish and for the international trade union movement.

CRISTINA: To be fair, that was no accident. Whenever privatisation and shock therapy were brought in, so many factories and shops couldn't have closed down if trade unions weren't weakened at the same time. Instead of standing together and walking out in protest, workers were made to feel fortunate when another colleague was let go. Legislation also changed to make strikes increasingly more difficult in Ireland, too. After Brexit, first there was Debenhams leaving Irish workers in the cold, then Iceland.

NORA: Something we've touched upon before is the neoliberal belief in individual solutions, like going out and consulting a solicitor yourself. I saw that uprooting this perspective, which many workers had previously believed to be the only approach to solving their grievances, was one of the main challenges to organising. And, relatedly, some workers' mistaken belief, at first, that the union is a service you pay for, like some kind of work insurance, rather than a collective endeavour you are part of and build yourself.

CRISTINA: We are now back to the issue where exhausted people will simply decide it's not worth the time or money to fight it, so they'll just leave for another job. While workers are encouraged to think of themselves as individuals with nothing in common, employers know that they need to stand together to defend their economic interests through the Irish Business and Employers Confederation (IBEC). What serves them is keeping working conditions just about the same in each workplace. That's why they campaign for policies that helps keep labour costs low—after all, the very name Human Resources suggests that workers are only as important as equipment. It's not a bug, it's a feature of the system.

NORA: It's this idea that you see with a lot of trade unions that if you have a problem, the only thing you can do is lodge a case with the WRC and wait to be heard out. No alternatives are discussed.

CRISTINA: Let's be honest, some issues simply can't wait, especially health and safety ones. For example, when Iceland remotely turned off the air conditioning in multiple locations but tried to excuse it as an environmental measure despite making it unsafe for their workers. Some issues are worth fighting for there and then.

NORA: This was especially urgent during the pandemic, when a lot of our activity was stunted by the lockdown just as their working conditions worsened. I was full of admiration for all the workers that showed the kind of enthusiasm you can only grow quickly by doing good work on the ground and listening to their issues. This means that, during the pandemic, we would meet 30 people in a park, but after the lockdown ended, that turned into 100 people attending a meeting.

What type of support did you need? What challenges did you face?

RÓISÍN: It took me a long time to realise how badly one needs a supportive partner and circle of friends to discuss the issues with. Before this realisation, emotional burnout is very real, and you feel like you must take all the work on without help. There is no shame in asking for help.

CRISTINA: It's all about trust, really. You need people you can safely ask for help, resources, or advice because you need to be very strategic when so many cards are stacked against you.

NORA: When I chose to join the IWU, I was happy with its radical, confrontational stance but worried about our limited resources, which affected recruitment and capacity. You would always see the same few members knocking on people's doors and doing the work, so like Róisín said, burnout is a real issue in this field. This is especially a risk if you are a woman, and you take on a lot of the emotional labour that is very time-consuming and draining that a lot of men either won't notice or won't do. When I was a CATU organiser, we'd have very dramatic cases and you'd support people round the clock, but it's difficult to break down the perception that you shouldn't let these things affect you or it's the women that should always handle it. Sometimes people dismiss these concerns by saying that emotional labour is not part of the job, and unions should not do it, but I fundamentally disagree. The reality is that we live in a society where access to mental health support is dismal, and where there is an amount of suffering and injustice that makes us all increasingly ill. If we do not find ways to collectivise and structure emotional supports within our struggles, we will either end up losing a lot of our best people who will simply not get the support they need to continue or end up having always the same organisers (usually not men) take up the emotional labour.

CRISTINA: You mentioned earlier being socialised to mediate. I'd like to also point out how often we are socialised to avoid drawing attention to ourselves, which can't help but make you feel conflicted as an organiser. Although you're not calling attention to yourself as a person, but in your role as organiser, you need to step up and speak up to call attention to the cause you're fighting for. Otherwise, issues are left to fester and become the new normal, while addressing them becomes unthinkable. This goes beyond having to fight the assumption that workers should shut up or seek better conditions elsewhere—it's also the perception that when women bring up an issue repeatedly until it gets solved, they're not determined, they're "nagging". It's been great to have the support of my colleagues in the IWU when navigating Irish law and industrial relations.

NORA: That's why I think it's important not to dismiss gendered issues in the workplace; they're not merely a secondary demand behind what everyone agrees on, like pay raises.

CRISTINA: Indeed, sometimes these are more immediate issues that would take less time. In a sense, not addressing many, seemingly minor issues is a kind of death by a thousand cuts, beating down workers who then think they have no power. On the other hand, if you get all the workforce behind one such issue in solidarity, you get an immediate win that improves morale and demonstrates that fighting back is achievable. Small, winnable, visible, deeply felt, and widely felt issues are the first to organise around.

NORA: Even if not directly affecting you, it affects a fellow worker and allowing them to be disrespected will spill over into you getting targeted next because the employer noticed your silence and the lack of opposition.

CRISTINA: An injury to one is an injury to all.

NORA: I think we can all agree on that!

What does the Irish trade union movement mean to you?

RÓISÍN: It has been an inspiration. Its historical roots with Jim Larkin, James Connolly, the Lockouts, and the women's movement in Belfast have all inspired and given me hope to get involved as much as possible with the work.

CRISTINA: When doing a programme in Irish Studies, I wrote a paper on James Connolly's work on and in the trade union movement, so it was very rewarding to go from theory to practice. It was obviously also a very different context by the time I came to Ireland, so I look at it as a movement that has great potential but needs to go back to prioritising bringing the fight to the employers.

NORA: What disappointed and disillusioned me about the Irish trade union movement was the active undermining of the IWU by other unions, which allowed themselves to be instrumentalised by management in the meat sector, just at the time we were starting to be successful in the meat plant union drive. Just as our organising started to pick up momentum in a factory, management would start claiming that they were not opposed to unionising per se, but that they would only accept another establishment union they had a prior agreement with. This was clearly a decoy as the other union that was suggested to the workers had never been present or done any organising in these workplaces for more than 20 years, and workers didn't even know it existed, and it was brought up only to delegitimise our own organising efforts. However, this said union never objected to being used as a worker control tool by meat plant management, even once they were explicitly made aware of this by IWU reps.

CRISTINA: It was disappointing when such an establishment union claimed that the workers could not choose which trade union to join despite no communication with them, almost like claiming subjects and a sphere of influence they believed they were entitled to.

NORA: I think the main objective of a trade union is to give the workers the resources to make demands themselves.

CRISTINA: I think we definitely all agree on this point, too!

What do you think about the Independent Workers' Union's place in the Irish trade union movement? What are your hopes and fears for its future?

RÓISÍN: Seeing the Iceland workers struggle and

interviewing the workers who stood up made me want to get involved with the Union. I think it plays a very important part, especially giving the working class tools in standing up for their rights. I believe it will continue to grow and protect workers.

CRISTINA: I agree, and I think it's important for the IWU to continue to dispel the idea that industrial relations are supposed to be too difficult to understand even though they affect us all.

NORA: As I was saying earlier and as Róisín also pointed out, my main hope for the IWU is to continue to help people become organisers themselves, skill up dedicated workers who organise on the ground, and encourage people of different political horizons to work together. This is something I have valued within CATU, where people many different political values but are able to work together effectively in tackling the housing crisis. I also feel there has to be an emphasis on democratic decision making and giving workers the confidence and information to be involved at all levels of the union.

CRISTINA: That's exactly where educational workshops come in. It's important to continue to see growth, especially after a successful first run of the Ray O'Reilly Winter School, where we were lucky to be joined by our friends in TradeMark. We have also passed a motion on organising a yearly Summer School, so the only way to go from now on is upwards and onwards.

❀

What advice do you have for other young women starting to become active in organising?

RÓISÍN: While I know when you walk into a meeting and you see you are the only woman there, you have to persist. I know it will be incredibly difficult, but if you are there, then you lead the way for more women to want to join. Keep on reading women activists and find support within your friendships with other women.

NORA: I agree. As a woman, you can still have trouble appearing legitimate to older men who may not want to listen to you and that can lead to you having a tendency to over apologise. You must stand your ground instead, because being conflict-avoidant only keeps the structures of power in place.

CRISTINA: Indeed, I'd say the main concern is to push through because organising work is a marathon, not a sprint. There is no point in waiting forever to fully prepare for it because without taking action, working conditions continue to deteriorate as we speak. We all have to pitch in the moment we can.

NORA: That's especially true for gendered issues. Be very vigilant about emotional work that is assigned but not valued and collectivise it where you can. If you exhaust yourself, it's no good for yourself or for the trade union movement.

CRISTINA: After all, you can't pour from an empty cup. Just like Róisín suggested, let's take this volume as an opportunity to engage with other women workers and trade union activists to replenish our cups together.

Interviews with Iceland Workers

Conducted in September and October 2023

Róisín Dubh

Aoife[1]

I have worked in retail for many years. I had been working [at] Iceland for five and a half years. I was in our store from day one. I have a small child. I had set up childcare around this job and had plans in place to save for a mortgage but that's all ruined now since being made redundant.

I have never been a part of a union and would love to get a job with IWU. I am a member, and I hate the injustice of it all. We got involved with IWU because of the way we're being treated by Metron[2] and Naeem Maniar[3] himself. Wages not being paid, and holidays being stolen from us. We

---

[1] Editor's note: Interviewee wished to remain anonymous, and a pseudonym was used for the sake of anonymity.

[2] Editor's note: Metron Stores Ltd. is the parent company of Iceland.

[3] Editor's note: Maniar is the new owner of Iceland.

had never needed outside help like a union until this company was taken over. Rob Metcalfe[4] and his team were always amazing to work for.

I have learned a lot that we have a voice, and it will be heard. I have also seen the more money you have the more you get away with. I hope something changes that people like Naeem Maniar can't buy businesses, run them into the ground as a tax dodge and get away with it.

My daughter keeps me going to stand up for ourselves. I want her to be proud of her mother that she sees we won't take it laying down.

Ironically, Iceland has always been a man's world run by men with male area managers dominantly male managers but yet the rest of the workers are mainly females. My own manager was a man but would never want to rock the boat and never stood up for us when we questioned wages or holiday pay. It was us women using our voices to be heard, reached out to the union for help.

This whole ordeal has deeply impacted me. I saw the highs and lows, made lifelong friends. I have in past, suffered with my mental health and going to work helped it. Gave me purpose, a connection to the outside world. Naeem Maniar never wanted Iceland to work, and the public need to know that.

---

4 Editor's note: Metcalfe is the former owner of Iceland

He didn't just run Iceland into the ground in a very short time. He took away our plans for the future. He has caused an immeasurable amount of stress and anxiety for all of us in a cost-of-living crisis, when all we wanted to do was go to work. I want him to know he is a coward and a bully and him and everyone of his henchmen should be ashamed of themselves.

The lesson that should be learned is that when you stick together the higher ups have to listen because together our voices are stronger.

Aishling

My name is Aishling, and I am forty-three years young. I'm a single mother to one child, and I have a mortgage on my own. I had been working four and half years for Iceland, and I was due sick pay in March (2023) and waited two weeks. I was never involved in a union before, but I joined the Union to help me get my money, although I am still waiting on that though.

I've learned it's best to fight for your rights and raising a child I want her to learn the value of not sitting back and allowing a company to treat you so unfairly for your right to work and be paid.

I've learned a lot from this experience both good and bad. I definitely recommend others to join a union. This country is a joke in my opinion to allow companies treat hard working Irish people the way we have is unreal. As my union rep would say, "stronger in numbers and stick together to fight the big bucks."

Thomas

My name is Thomas, and I'm 26 years old. I live with my family, went to secondary school, and live in Ballybane. I worked at Iceland for almost 6 years.

I got involved with the IWU because I heard how workers were being treated by the company and felt like I should stand up. Before the IWU I've never been involved in a union. From this situation I learned that people are genuinely stronger together and if we want to get something done we have to stand together. I hope people learn from this situation that standing together isn't futile, even if it's against people who put money above their own staff and have little to no morals.

Alex Homits definitely inspired me to join

the IWU in the first place, getting to talk to him in person inspired me to keep going too. People like him are rare, I can tell he has strong morals.

The IWU already understands the power of people standing in solidarity, but I hope we never forget or underestimate that power we have. Too often greedy money hungry people, like the heads of the company try to take advantage of workers so I hope we never forget how powerful a workers union actually is.

Saoirse[5]

I am 21 years old, and I support my family paying bills and rent. I was working in Iceland for 4 years, and I got involved in the IWU as we had not been in a union previously as we hadn't had issues before. I am owed a large amount of money myself from missing wages and holiday pay.

This was my first job I was not in a union before all this. I joined the IWU to fight for what we were and still are owed. I think the Union have done everything for us. The support we have from them is absolutely amazing.

---

5 Editor's note: Interviewee wished to remain anonymous

I was a store manager and although I am owed money. I continued fighting for staffs' wages that have still not been paid to them. I can't understand how they can be so rude we didn't get told anything. They[6] sent workers in one of the days, and they started measuring the chillers. I walked down and asked who they were, and he was able to tell me we were getting new chillers[7] put it. These were also rented which weren't paid as the chiller company rang the store as the bill wasn't paid, the rent was also not paid as the landlord came to the store asking for head offices number as he wasn't even informed of the takeover. I believe UK Iceland are in on this as Naeem was able to tell us that "METRON" stood for Ron Metcalfe, who works in Northern Ireland. Their Homesavers managers and head office people were in our store since March.

Caitriona was store manager of Homesavers[8] Ballyfermot and was put into our store when our manager was pushed out for sticking up for us on our missing wages only in the second week. Katie is Homesavers merchandise, who opens and closes stores, was also in our store for 2 months. They also

---

6 Editor's note: Iceland Owners

7 Editor's note: Refrigerators that contain chilled food, milk, and meats

8 Editor's note: Another company owned by the owners of Iceland

sent Kevin and Gary, who are Homesavers managers into Talbot Street Iceland, and Jenny into both Talbot Street and Ballyfermot. Jeff and Naeem[9] would walk into the store and completely ignore all of us. As I was told by a Homesavers manager to let them walk first and to "never say no to Jeff" when he tells you to do something. I had two cases against them yet I've still not heard anything with the WRC.[10]

What I've took from all this is no matter how much you may do for them you won't be appreciated. I will stay in the union. It affected me on so many levels as bills would fail to come out as they paid me wrong, and then I owed late fees and having to get lends of money to live which I'm still paying back.

Debbie

I support myself and my husband, and I am 53 years old. My family has a history of union workers, my dad and sisters were in a union. I was not able to turn to my father for advice, as he passed away, and

---

9 Editor's note: Iceland owners

10 Editor's note: Workplace Relations Committee. A government entity that handles labor disputes against companies.

my sisters live in different parts of the country, and we only speak occasionally. I was not in a union before this dispute. I worked at Iceland for 15 Years before the strike.

Alex came into my store in Tallaght at the start of the dispute and I knew the union was the only way we would be heard as the Company was ignoring anything we said to them. From this, I learned that the only way we were heard was through our union as these cowboys belittled us and ignored anything we put to them. I learned that you have to stand up for yourself and make our voices heard, because the big boys don't always win and every voice deserves to be heard.

My husband, family, and friends inspired me to keep going. I'm not a mother myself, but some of my work colleagues are, and I have seen the impact this had on them. They said they were doing this so their children would know that women have a voice to and it needs to be heard.

I don't think we would be where we are today without our union as these cowboys would not listen to a word we said. I would like to thank the IWU and especially Alex who fought every step of the way for the Iceland Workers. I will stay involved with this Union and continue to be a paying member of the union. I will keep putting my views across, when need be, to help other people in our situation.

DONNA

I am a 32-year-old mother of one. My son is 10, and has additional needs, I have a degree in social care, and I originally was a homecare support worker before working at Iceland. I have a wide range of experience in social care, youth work, and different exchange programmes.

I don't have a history of union workers in my family. However, during my volunteering in youth work I learned a lot about the importance of being in a union in order to be fairly represented.

I had been working in Iceland for 2 and ½ years, but for me Iceland was more than a job, it was a place where we went to work. Everyone got on. Our staff team was very supportive of each other. We could always depend on each other, and we had great relationships built up with our customers also.

I had never been involved with a union, but I got involved with the IWU when changes happened in the store, and when the store was put on temporary pay off which in turn ended in permanent closure.

I've learned the importance of standing up for our rights. Basic human rights are to be treated with equality dignity and respect. Evidently this wasn't the case for the Iceland workers in each store. Therefore, the occupation of Talbot Street allowed us to stand up for all workers, to stand up for the rights of employees, and to not let people treat us in this way again.

I hope that people learn this can happen to any workplace or work environment. Nobody's jobs are safe when employers can treat employees how we were treated. I hope workers see the action we have taken and stand up for their rights. I hope workers join unions and support each other.

I think the union have been amazing all the way through. They did everything in their power to support us every step of the way, and we will forever be grateful to them. We met some amazing people as a result of this actions, and we gained a lot of knowledge and experience from the union.

I would like to highlight the importance of supporting each other in a situation like this action. I think when everyone stands together, supports, and motivates each other well, then it shows real solidarity. I've gained so much form the action and the occupation of our store that I'll carry with me for life.

Trades Unions and Women's Employment

First Published in *The Irish Citizen*
December 11, 1915

Mary Galway

Before I proceed to deal with the subject matter of my paper on Trade Unionism, I propose to sketch briefly for your information the conditions prevailing in the mills and factories in Belfast, where then, as now, women and girls form 95 percent of the total workers employed. Wages were deplorable small, fines were outrageous, the workers being penalised in various sums and often dismissed for trifles, and very often the mistakes were due, not to the incapacity or carelessness of the workers, but to defective machinery or bad material supplied. Moreover, there was no security of employment, and the worker did not know the moment she would find herself outside the gate, very often with no clear idea of why she had been dismissed. The sanitary conditions were also deplorable, there being dry W.C.'s in some of the largest factories in Belfast, very often with no ventilation or ventilators kept closed, so that the workrooms were hot-beds of disease. The overheating of weaving sheds, which frequently had a temperature of between 80 and 90 degrees, was also inimical to the health of the workers in the Summer time, when there were numerous case of fainting. These conditions led to the formation of the Textile Operatives' Society, by the Belfast Trades Council, at the suggestion of Lady Dilke, who, while in Belfast attending the British Trade Union Congress, held in Belfast in September, 1893, took advantage of the opportunity to investigate the conditions then prevailing in the Linen Trade, and came to the conclusion that in the union of workers would lie their strength.

It was certainly a remarkable thing that it was left to an American lady to better the lot of Irish women and girls.

The task of organising women in Ireland is one of extreme difficulty. You must remember that Irish girls are not brought up in a Trade Union atmosphere, as boys in well organised trades are; the girl never hears Trade Unionism as it affects herself and her sex discussed, because her mother and grandmother had no Trade Union in their day, and therefore know nothing about it. We often find when girls are asked to join the Union they do not know any of the advantages, while in some cases the mother, when asked her opinion in the matter, says "there was no such thing in my young days, and we got along right well without it." They don't seem to take into account the changed conditions under which then younger generations work. Another great drawback to the organising women is the very tender age at which girls have been, and are being put to work, with little or no education, and no means of improving, and by such improvement learning what Trade Unionism has done in all countries where the workers have been wise enough to organise. Again, the domestic duties which falls to the lot of most girls, alter the daily work in mills and factories, leaves no time to study the barometer which indicates the rise in wages and improvement in conditions of work with the development of Trade Unionism.

I regret to say that I have found that the first flush of enthusiasm for organising sometimes almost as quickly evaporates, for instance, during the great strike of mill and factory workers, for an advance of wages, which occurred in 1906, we received about 5,000 names of women and girls, but after a month's constant hard work in arranging the names into districts and visiting the homes of the workers by an earnest and energetic band of workers, not more than 9000 became full-fledged members. Again, many members pay for a few weeks and then stop without giving any reason at all, except that they cannot be bothered paying the contributions, although our district collectors call at the homes of the members each week for the contributions, a contrast to many men's Unions, where members have to attend at the clubroom each week and wait their turn in order to pay their dues. One of the most serious obstacles, however, to the progress of our Union, has been the opposition of employers. It is easy to understand why so many hundreds of women and girls, knowing that their weekly wage is all that stands between them and starvation, are terrified to do anything that might deprive them, even for one week, of that wage. I know for a fact that cases are occurring every day where women have to hide from their employers the knowledge that they are members of our Union, for they know that the moment that such knowledge reaches the employers, some excuse would be found for dismissing them. In one instance, namely, at Dromore, Co. Down, a new Branch established on the occasion of a strike was broken up by the factory manager dismissing some of the workers who acted as officers of the Branch, while at Monkstown, Co. Antrim, where there was a strike, one of the employer's friends was good enough to offer any two women in the village the magnificent sum of 5s. each if they would immerse me in the mill-dam. The friend was saved the 5s. expense, as the women, perhaps thinking the physical exertion more than they were able for, did not attempt to carry out the suggestion. So great is the anxiety of some of our members to hide their association with the Union, that they are even afraid to tell their fellow-workers of their membership. Not withstanding all these difficulties I think we can claim that the Society has fully justified its existence, and been the means of greatly ameliorating the conditions which prevailed when it was brought into being. I think you will agree with this claim when you hear a few extracts from our Annual Reports, such extracts being based on absolutely incontrovertible evidence. The facts not only showing the benefits accruing to the members, but also shedding some light on the moral principles, or rather lack of these, on the part of the employers.

Increases in Wages

In 1903, 100 piro-winders struck work against a differentiation of pay in two fo the local factories. The workers appealed to me, as Secretary of the Society, and after negotiations with the Company the workers received the amount asked for, namely, 1s. per week increase, which they are still receiving. In the same year 42 warp-winders struck work on account of bad material. They claimed this work required a higher rate of pay, and after negotiations with the Company they received the amount claimed, 8d per week, which amount they are still in receipt of. 100 weavers struck against a production of wages, and after a fortnight's strike I succeeded in having, not only the reduction withdrawn, but an increase given, which amounted to 2s. per week, and the deductions made previous to the strike refunded. On looking over my reports I find that on an average of four advances per year have been gained for different classes of workers, and in response to a deputation of representatives from the various Unions of Belfast and District, a general advance of 3 percent, was obtained for all employees in the Linen Trade.

Fines

In 1902, a member of the Textile Society, a hem-stitcher, was fined in the sum of thirty shillings for alleged faults in her work. Such faults were due, she maintained, to insufficient instructions, and on my advice she refused to pay the fine, and was kept on by the firm, which as a proof that she was a competent worker. Afterwards she was fined again, and refused to pay, with the result she was dismissed without notice, discharge paper, or wages. She reported the matter to me, and I instructed our solicitor to issue a summons for 10s, wages in lieu of notice, 8s. 6d. wages earned, and discharge. The employer paid up the sum mentioned and costs and gave discharge.

In 1912, a damask worker of forty years experience was fined 10s. for alleged faults in a piece of line damask. She refused to allow the deduction to be made, on the ground that the yarn supplied was of inferior quality. The employer, however, insisted in taking the fine from her wages. She then applied to me, and I put her case in the hands of our solicitor. When the Company learned that the Society had taken up the case, they refunded the fine, 10s. paid all wages due and costs. On an average we have had four of such cases each year, but we have had innumerable cases where smaller fines were returned at once when the Society intervened, while our action at the outset and later has had such a deterrent effect that there is not one line now for every twenty inflicted formerly.

The Society's action in this direction was not confined to the cases mentioned above, and we invoked the aid of the Home Office in the matter. So serious did they consider the grievances of the weavers in a factory outside of Belfast, that they sent their Senior Labour Adviser to the Board of Trade, Mr. D. J. Shackleton, and the Chief Lady Inspector of Factories, Miss A. Anderson, to investigate my complaint. I cannot do better than quote the following extract, based on the result of this investigation, from the Annual Report of 1911 of the Chief Inspector of Factories, which says: - "In one factory I found 65,763 of the weavers were fined an average find of 8 3/4d. per week, the average net wage being 3s. 81/2d. per week, and the evil evidently tended to grow, as six months earlier only 60.3 of the weavers were fined an average fine of 7 1/2d. per week. In spite of warnings by Mr. Shackleton, and by myself, that this could not go on, Miss Slocock (a Lady Inspector) reported to me in 1912 that the percentage of weavers fined had risen to 83 percent. Let me summarise what followed. A threat to prosecute brought reform, teachers were appointed, and when the factory was revisited later it was found that the percentage of weavers fined had fallen from 83 percent to 6.9 percent, and the average fine was 6d.

Accidents

A member of our Society, employed as a damask weaver, injured her right arm while turning the handle of her loom, thereby breaking the muscles. The employer paid her 7s. 4d. per week, about half her average earnings, for some months, and when she refused to go to hospital, stopped the payments. The Society took the case to court, and upon the woman agreeing to go to hospital, the deferred compensation was paid, and later the firm settled the case by giving the worker £90 and all costs. The worker admitted to me that without the assistance of the Society she could not have fought the employers.

Another member, while engaged as a spinner, fell, injuring her leg. She was taken to hospital, when she remained for two months, during which time the employer made no move to pay her compensation. The Society took the matter up, and succeeded in getting her 4s. 9d. per week, half her average earnings. This amount was paid to her for three years, when her employer settled the case, after a hard fight on the part of the Society, and paid the woman £79 and costs. When I tell you that this woman was 38 years in the employment of this Company, you will have some idea of the type of employers we, as a Society, have to deal with in the linen trade.

A third member, employed as a weaver, fell in a factory, sustaining an injury to her left knee-cap. She was paid half her average wages, 3s. 10d. per week, for about 8 weeks, when the employer ceased payment. The Society took the case to court, and compelled the Company to continue the payments. This went on for three and a half years, during which time the Company stopped payments on three different occasions, but each time we took the case to court and won again, then the Company settled the matter by paying the worker £130 and costs, which added to the half pay for three and half years, meant a sum of over £200. This worker was 37 years in the employment of this firm. You will thus see that BELFAST IS ONE OF THE VERY FEW PLACES WHERE LONG SERVICE HAS NO REWARD.

Another feature of the work of the Trade Union, in looking after the welfare of women and girls, was to see that the internal arrangements of the mills and factories were safe and conducive to the health of the workers. In this connection I lodged with the Factory Inspectors an average of 30 complaints each year regarding bad sanitary arrangements, machinery not being properly fenced, overheating and violations of the Truck and Factory Acts. The complaints were duly investigated, and the evils complained of remedied.

The Society did not confine its activities to Belfast, but extended its operations to Londonderry, Newry, Dromore, Banbridge, Lisburn, Lurgan, Portadown, Monkstown, Whiteabbey, and Whitehouse in Ulster, and to Drogheda and Kilkenny in Leinster. In fact, wherever there was a slightest indication on the part of the workers in any part of the country to organise, we were at their service at once. You will thus see that the Textile Operatives' Society of Ireland has achieved something on behalf of the workers of Ireland. I may also state that, after 12 years strenuous exertion on our part, the Government at last recognised the importance of the work done by our Society, and rising to a sense of its duty, appointed the first Resident Lady Inspector of Factories for Ireland in 1909, and although this was a step in the right direction, it was totally inadequate, as one lady, no matter how energetic, could not be expected to thoroughly inspect all the factories and workshops in Ireland.

Other evidence came to me to show that the Government appreciated the work done by our Union, as I was called to give evidence before a Committee appointed by the House of Commons in 1908 to consider the Truck Act, and also as a witness before the Departmental Committee, appointed by the House of Commons in 1909 to investigate accidents in mills and factories, and again as a witness before the Committee appointed by the Home Office in 1911, to consider the question of what is known as Shuttle-kissing in factories (a source of spreading disease), and as a witness before the Committee appointed to inquire into sweating among the outworkers in the linen trade in 1912. As the result of these inquiries many most valuable reforms have been introduced, and the lot of the worker more tolerable.

Although the work has been uphill, and at times very disheartening, it has had its compensation in the knowledge that it improved the miserable lot of so many women and girls, not only in the linen trade, but in many other occupations, where, although the workers were not members of our Union, we willingly lent them a helping hand in all difficulties by giving them advice, and thereby enabling them to secure justice, which, previous to the formation of our Union, was very often denied them.

If the present war has taught us one thing more than another, it is that no Empire can hope to succeed without the wholehearted cooperation of the masses now being exhibited on the battlefield abroad and in the workshops. I sincerely hope when peace is once more restored, and when we begin to create a new social system, based on the mournful experience of the past 16 months, a bridge will be erected to unite for all time to come the classes and the masses of our dear country, and that, incidentally, the Government will set itself the task of looking better after the working classes, especially the women and girls, so that the next generation may live in a purer, sweeter, and more enabling atmosphere.

"Woman's Place": Home or Factory? The Limits of Change

First Published in *Labour News* December 19, 1936

Nora Connolly O'Brien

There has been of late much irritating talk on the subject of "Women in Industry"; of women in industry driving men out of employment, of the dangerous moral and physical effects of allowing women to tend machines in factories. Talk—by intelligent men—so much up in the air, ignoring the root causes for women being in factories, and men out of them, that it behoves one of that realistic section of the nation, women, to put forward a few facts for consideration.

The industrialisation of the world put an end for all time to the idea—and made claptrap of the phrase—that "woman's place is in the home." Prior to the industrial era all industries were home industries. There were then no gigantic bakeries employing strong trade union men at making machine bread. The woman made the bread in her home—it occupied some of her time. If intelligent men began to talk about a law compelling women to make bread at home what an outcry there would be, and if such a law was passed how many thousands of men would be unemployed?

Closing Factories

If women were compelled by law to buy pigs and cure the family's supply of bacon, how many bacon factories would be closed and how many more men would be unemployed? And if looms were erected in every home to weave material for clothes, blankets, sheets, tablecloths and rugs, how many more factories would close and how many more men would be unemployed? If every home kept its own hens, if every house made its own butter, what would happen to our creameries and egg distributors and then men they employ? If every house knit its own socks, stockings, boys' jerseys, jumpers, pullovers and woollen underwear what would happen to the men who make the machinery for knit goods, who build the factories for making those machines, and the factories to house the machinery, and make crate to hold the finished goods, and the men who dispatch the goods, and the railwaymen who carry them, and the commercial men who sell them, and the men in the building trades who build the shops to sell them, and the shop fitters who enable them to be displayed? Why continue? You can apply the same question to the majority of the necessities of life which used to occupy woman's time when her place was in the home.

If it were possible for women to retire to their homes—*but it is not!*—civilisation as we know it, based on industrial development, would come crashing down, business would be in chaos if women were to be excluded from factories.

Realist's View

Think the matter out clearly. This is no mere feminist or Labour point of view. It is a realist's point of view. It is a facing of facts. The whole industrial life of any country now is based upon the fact that the acts of housewifery are more quickly and economically carried out by machinery than by the work of the individual women of the community, and the inventive genius of man for generations has been directed to producing monster machines to further that idea, so that now the home as it used to be and women's work in the home is like Othello's occupation—gone.

If women are expelled from industry, what are they to do? How occupy their time? Much more important, how are they to exist? Experience has taught us that our benevolent employers are not willing to give more than a subsistence wage to a man with which he is expected to keep himself, his wife and growing family. What is he to do if his growing family is composed of daughters, and they insist upon growing up? Will our benevolent employers increase a man's wages as his daughters grow up, so that his wage will be sufficient to feed, clothe, house and provide relaxation for an adult female family? And if a man dies or becomes incapacitated, will the same employer provide the necessary means of subsistence for his adult female family?

If our employers do not, what are the females of our race to do? And if, oh, miracle of miracles! they do, what can the women find to occupy their time?

Let there be no foolish talk of attending to the home, or training themselves to take care of a house or family.

With 30,000 families living in one room in Dublin—the name becomes a mockery, a place to get out of in order that one woman may find space to attempt neatness, tidiness, cooking, washing and mending. Imagine two or three or four women trying to occupy themselves in such a confined space! The irritation consequent upon the attempt would develop such an epidemic of nervous disorders that the main occupation of the men could well become the certifying, driving to, and receiving women in lunatic asylums. And those who saved their sanity by being driven to the streets by idleness, what of the dangers to their moral and physical well-being? The industrial world will not change even if women are driven from industry, save that more perfect machines will be invented needing less to attend them, but turning out in far greater quantities those things which in pre-industrial era women occupied themselves in producing when their place was in the home.

No Homes

They who deplore the falling marriage rate ignore the fact that present-day civilisation provides no homes for newly-married couples in Ireland. The ordinary workingman and woman who desire to marry have no prospect of a home save a room in a slum. Our Christian municipalities having decreed that slum clearance shall be a staple Irish industry, in a few years there would be no large families to be cleared out of slums if newly-married couples were not compelled to spend the first ten years in them.

A. de Blacam made a ludicrous suggestion lately that women should confine themselves to the teaching and nursing professions. Surely he is aware that there are hundreds of teachers qualified each year who can find no class to teach. That is a fact now, while teachers are given the impossible task of teaching classes of 50, 60, and sometimes more. How can any teacher be expected, or ever hope, to give the rudiments of education to children in such classes? Why should women give years to training when the Government can't or won't supply schools that can employ enough teacher to prepare children to receive education? Is the prospect of getting a job so rosy that working-class families should make the necessary sacrifices to have all their girls trained as teachers? Ask the teachers' organisation! Today the industry of making teachers is suffering from over-production, too!

Teachers and Nurses

And as for nursing a girl of a working class or small farmer family who desires to be a nurse is compelled to emigrate to England in order to be trained. Irish hospitals demand a big fee, and the family must keep the girl in clothes, pocket and entertainment money during the years of training. English hospitals ask no fee and pay a graduated salary during training, which relieves the strain on the girl's family.

But can A. de Blacam visualise the nation in which all its unmarried women are occupied as teachers and nurses? To keep them employed, wouldn't it be necessary to be a nation of invalids and children?

Don't let us be carried away by this talk of women in industry being responsible for so much of men's unemployment. It is a red herring to draw men off the scent. Unemployment of men is not caused by the employment of women. It is caused by the capitalist system of production for profit. Capitalists have employed women in industry because they have found them more profitable. Women do not work for lower wages than men because they like them better, but because they have to take them or starve. Equal pay for equal work will end the abuse of women in industry.

Equal Pay

Every Labour Party and every Trades Union Congress has had that slogan on its programme for a long time. But there does not seem much chance of having it put into effect. Without a terrific change in men's mentality. I can't imagine a strike by men to compel an employer to pay a man's wage to a woman, but I can imagine at the present moment (and whisper, I've even heard) men Trades Unionists approve of the idea of women's exclusion from industry.

And I've heard intelligent men talk of the monotonous drudgery of women tending machines, and asking that they be saved from it by law, but I've never heard one of them ask for a law to compel that only men should be employed at the monotonous drudgery of charring.

Let us be sensible. We can't solve the unemployment problem by displacing one section of workers by another. If women were excluded from industry there would still be an unemployment problem running into the hundred thousands. And it is quite possible that dissatisfied, discontented ordinary women with no outlet could well be a greater danger to those who uphold the present system, and suggest their disemployment in order to temporarily satisfy discontented men.

Tinkering is no use. The only satisfactory solution to the unemployment problem is to end production for profit, when there will be equal pay for equal work. When that is achieved there will be no time wasted in useless discussion on "Women in Industry."

Two Roads for Irishwomen

First Published in *The Irishman* July 14, 1917

Maud Eden

We are at a crisis in Irish history. We must act upon principle, adapt one line of conduct, and stick to that alone!

Today, two lines of conduct are open to Irish women, particularly working women. They may fight for Irish freedom or they may accept "English gold."

"Trade Unioinism" has lately made great strides among English women. When war came, and men were recruited and conscripted, their sisters and sweethearts came forward and kept war going by doing their work. A grateful Government increased their pay. Arbitration Tribunals raised gold on the women workers who made possible war and conscription. Just as the Separation ladies are prosperous in our midst. 'Tis true there are some complaints about morals! But what of that. Today, a great opportunity awaits Irish women. Certain benevolent ladies, notably Miss S. C. Harrison, inspired no doubt by a benevolent Government, have brought over here an English "Federation" Organiser. Luckily the existence of the Irish Women Workers' Union has prevented the plot going as well as was at first intended. The English Federation has been obliged to confine its attention to Munition Workers, though an organiser was originally invited over to deal with all classes of women workers. The first intimation we got about Miss Harrison's arrangements was hearing she had asked the Trades' Council to lend her a room for a meeting They refused!

I suggest that Irish working women should put the following questions to Miss S. C. Harrison and her English friends—(1) Is she or is she not opposed to Industrial Conscription? (2) If Industrial Conscription is attempted here, does she intend to advise Dublin working women to obey the law, or to resist it tooth and nail? (3) Is she prepared to face death and imprisonment in the cause of the Revolutionary Movement?

If Irish women accept Miss Harrison as their leader, they will no doubt get temporary increases in wages, which they will lose when their masters are again strong enough to take them away. If they acknowledge English Unions and take English Trades' Union money, they are selling the cause of Irish freedom. English Labour people will believe that Irish men and Irish women are too lazy, ignorant and helpless to manage their own Irish Labour Movement. If we are Unionists, let us act as Unionists; if Separationists, let us keep separate from England. If we dislike English domination in politics, why accept it in Labour affairs!

Irish women will get good pay temporarily if they will kindly enable employers to dismiss men. Will Irish girls sell their lovers and brothers for the sake of higher wages? English women have sold their men's lives and their own souls for increased wages. Will Irish women do the same? Never! Let us stick to the Labour Movement founded by James Connolly, and we will soon have no need to beg for English aid in the management of our own affairs.

Countess de Markievicz is with us once more. All over Ireland, awakened womanhood claims her as leader! Who can doubt that she will lead us by the path of National freedom to a state of National prosperity under our own laws?

Are Irish women to be free citizens of a free Ireland, electing their own representatives to control their own destinies, or poor, meek wage salves, humbly accepting bounty from Society ladies and

English "Labour"? English gold, English Unions, English Arbitration and English Wage Boards will bring with them English morals! What moral standards have these English Trade Unionists? Do they tolerate on their executives people openly practising free love? What has the English "federation" done to give moral protection to Irish girls in England?

The Irish Women Workers' Union has opened an Office at 18 Dame Street, Dublin, and will be glad to receive new members there.

NOTES:

Notes:

www.ingramcontent.com/pod-product-compliance
Lightning Source LLC
LaVergne TN
LVHW092104060526
838201LV00047B/1567